History's Greatest Mysteries

HISTORY'S ANCIENT AND MEDIEVAL SECRETS

by Grace Hansen

abdobooks.com

Published by Pop!, a division of ABDO, PO Box 398166, Minneapolis, Minnesota 55439. Copyright © 2023 by Abdo Consulting Group, Inc. International copyrights reserved in all countries. No part of this book may be reproduced in any form without written permission from the publisher. DiscoverRoo™ is a trademark and logo of Pop!.

Printed in the United States of America, North Mankato, Minnesota.

052022
092022

THIS BOOK CONTAINS RECYCLED MATERIALS

Cover Photos: Getty Images; Shutterstock Images

Interior Photos: Shutterstock Images; Getty Images; Charles Earnest Butler; Granger Collection

Editor: Elizabeth Andrews
Series Designer: Candice Keimig

Library of Congress Control Number: 2021951853

Publisher's Cataloging-in-Publication

Names: Hansen, Grace, author.

Title: History's ancient and medieval secrets / by Grace Hansen

Description: Minneapolis, Minnesota : Pop, 2023 | Series: History's greatest mysteries | Includes online resources and index

Identifiers: ISBN 9781098242268 (lib. bdg.) | ISBN 9781644947890 (pbk.) | ISBN 9781098242961 (ebook)

Subjects: LCSH: History, Ancient--Juvenile literature. | History, Medieval--Juvenile literature. | Curiosities and wonders--Juvenile literature.

Classification: DDC 942.03--dc23

WELCOME TO DiscoverRoo!

Pop open this book and you'll find QR codes loaded with information, so you can learn even more!

Scan this code* and others like it while you read, or visit the website below to make this book pop!

popbooksonline.com/anc-med-secrets

*Scanning QR codes requires a web-enabled smart device with a QR code reader app and a camera.

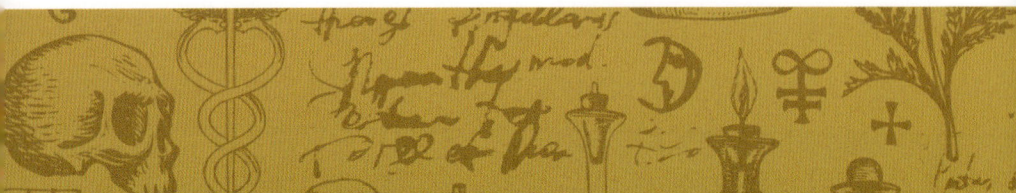

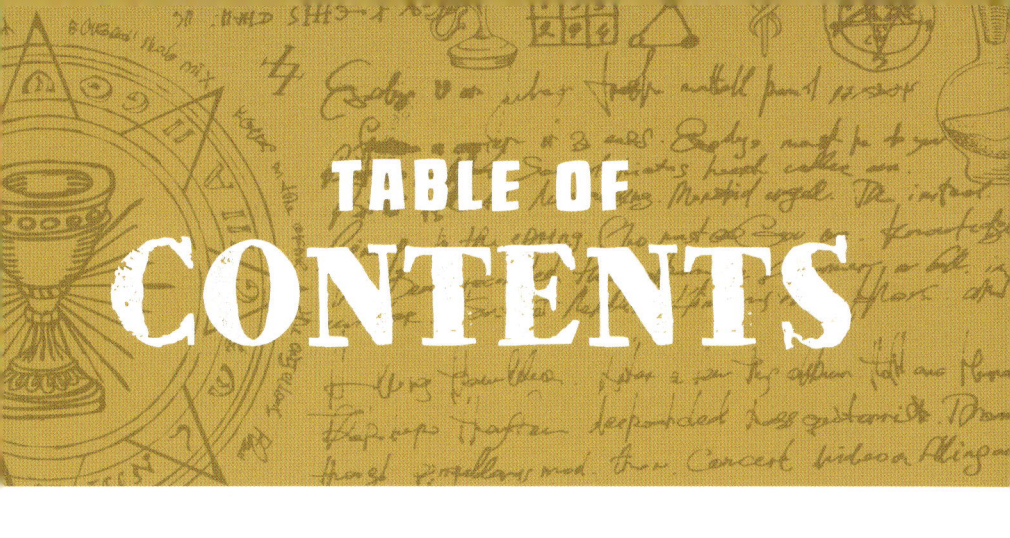

TABLE OF CONTENTS

CHAPTER 1
Hidden Secrets 4

CHAPTER 2
Where Is Cleopatra? 6

CHAPTER 3
King Arthur: Legendary
Fact or Fiction? 14

CHAPTER 4
Princes in the Tower 20

Making Connections. 30
Glossary 31
Index. 32
Online Resources 32

CHAPTER 1

HIDDEN SECRETS

Mysteries from ancient and medieval times continue to puzzle historians. Recorded information was lucky to survive long enough for us to find. Even with such luck, researchers must dig for evidence that people left behind.

WATCH A VIDEO HERE!

Though there are clues in things like ancient Egyptian **hieroglyphics** and medieval manuscripts, the questions we have might never be answered.

Clues to the mysteries of the past are hidden in places like ancient Egyptian tombs.

CHAPTER 2

WHERE IS CLEOPATRA?

Perhaps the most powerful woman to walk the earth was Cleopatra. Though she lived 2,000 years ago, her name is known well today. What remains a mystery is her final resting place. Cleopatra VII was the last true **pharaoh** of ancient Egypt, a society famous for its **mummies**.

LEARN MORE HERE!

Cleopatra was of Greek descent. She learned the Egyptian language and worked to protect Egypt from the Roman Empire. She was a very popular ruler.

Cleopatra was a poet who spoke many languages. She was well-studied in politics, mathematics, and economics. At just 18, she took control of Egypt after her father's death.

Cleopatra related herself to the goddess Isis, a protector of women. Vultures, like the one seen here on Cleopatra's head, were symbols of maternal protection.

The Battle of Actium took place on September 2 in 31 BCE.

In 31 BCE, the Roman Senate declared war against Cleopatra. After a disastrous defeat at the Battle of Actium off the coast of Greece, Cleopatra retreated to Egypt. There, in 30 BCE, historians believe she made an **asp** bite her. She died at the age of 39.

Cleopatra tested many poisons. She found that death by asp poison was the least terrible way to die.

Like all important Egyptians, Cleopatra's body would have been prepared and mummified. She would have been buried somewhere important surrounded by riches for the afterlife. **Scholars** believed that Cleopatra was buried in Alexandria, a city that was lost to the Mediterranean Sea more than a thousand years ago. Still, that has not stopped archaeologists from searching for her remains for centuries.

DID YOU KNOW?

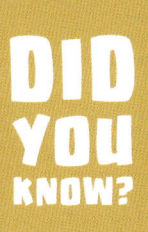

It is believed that the ancient Egyptians gave mummies golden tongues so the dead could speak to gods in the afterlife.

Dr. Kathleen Martinez came up with a new theory. She said the Egyptian ruler would never have wanted the Romans to find her tomb, and so Cleopatra carefully planned and "outsmarted everyone."

Dr. Kathleen Martinez is a lawyer and archaeologist.

Since 2004, Martinez and a team have been digging up a temple for the god Osiris and goddess Isis called Taposiris Magna. Her work has uncovered artifacts from the time Cleopatra lived, including coins decorated with Cleopatra's face. In 2021, the team found many tombs. Inside were mummies with golden tongues. Even more exciting was the discovery of a funeral mask and a decorated case holding a female mummy. Only time will tell if Martinez has solved one of history's greatest mysteries.

THINGS YOU MIGHT FIND IN A PHARAOH'S TOMB

Four canopic jars holding the lungs, liver, intestines, and stomach

Clothing, jewelry, and treasures

Wall paintings

A sarcophagus

CHAPTER 3

KING ARTHUR: LEGENDARY FACT OR FICTION?

King Arthur is the central character in a collection of tales and medieval romances known as the Matter of Britain. Legend has it that the king bravely led British forces into battle in the late 5th or early 6th century.

COMPLETE AN ACTIVITY HERE!

King Arthur was a legendary British leader.

Most scholars agree that the Battle of Badon took place in southern England sometime around 500 CE.

In around 400 CE the last Roman soldiers left Britain. The country was without a strong army to protect it from invaders. The **Anglo-Saxons** were just one group to take advantage of Britain's weakness. The **Britons** did put up a fight though.

The Battle of Badon is one supposed example. *The History of the Britons* by Nennius tells of King Arthur leading the **cavalry charge** in the 12th battle for Britain. From that one charge, 960 Anglo-Saxons fell. It is said that the victory halted the Saxon expansion for many years, making Arthur a beloved hero.

DID YOU KNOW? Disney's *The Sword in the Stone* is based on legends of King Arthur. In the movie, a wizard named Merlin helps a poor, young Arthur realize his royal path.

Early texts inspired writers to create grander tales surrounding Arthur. One such story has stood the test of time: *The Sword in the Stone*. The Arthurian legend says a stone and its sword rested in London. The sword could only be removed by the rightful king of Britain. When Arthur was sent to fetch a sword for his half-brother Kay, he unknowingly pulled the mighty weapon from the stone and became king.

A drawing of King Arthur by Howard Pyle, 1903

King Arthur makes for an exciting character, but was he real? Debate has gone on for hundreds of years. Though they have tried, historians cannot confirm whether he ever existed. But some say it's possible. Arthur may have been based off a Roman military leader who helped defend Britain. Another theory suggests Arthur was based off many real leaders of the time. In any case, the thrilling tales of King Arthur will continue to entertain the masses for years to come.

CHAPTER 4
PRINCES IN THE TOWER

Long after King Arthur's alleged battles for Britain came The Wars of the Roses (1455-85). These were a series of civil wars fought between two families for the throne of England. King Henry VI led the House of Lancaster, symbolized by the red rose. The House of York, represented by a white rose, was headed by Henry's cousin Edward IV.

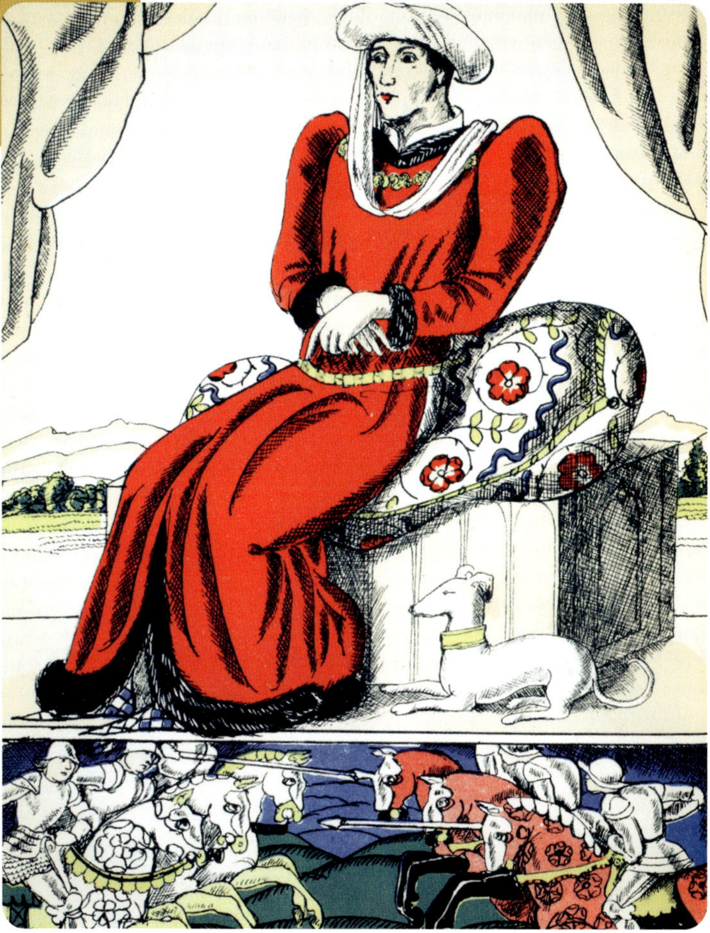

Henry VI was the King of England from 1422-1461 and then again from 1470-1471.

PRUNED FAMILY TREES OF LANCASTER AND YORK

HOUSE OF LANCASTER

- Henry VI
- Margaret of Anjou

Edward of Westminster, Prince of Wales

 # HOUSE OF YORK

Richard of York — Cicily Neville

Edward IV — Elizabeth Woodville | Richard III — Anne Neville

Richard | **Edward V** | **Edward of Middleham, Prince of Whales**

The Tower of London still stands in the city today.

Edward IV became king in 1471 when Henry VI died while imprisoned in the Tower of London. The former king's death was not a natural one, however. He was murdered. And the prime suspect was Edward's brother, Richard III. When King Edward IV fell ill in the spring of 1483, Richard III waged a quiet war against his own family.

Edward V, only 12, became king upon his father's death. His uncle Richard III was named Lord Protector. For his safety, Edward was sent to live in the Tower of London until his **coronation**. Soon Edward's only brother, Richard, joined him.

The princes, and heirs to the throne, were kept in the Tower of London.

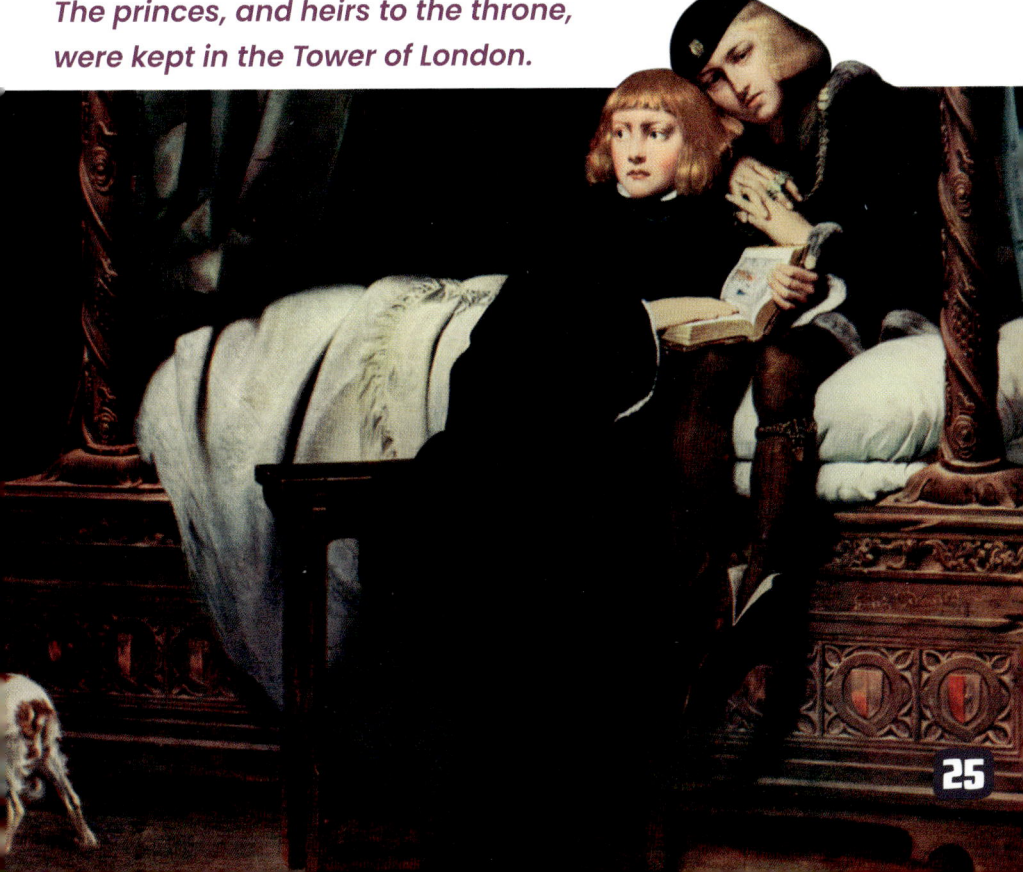

Supposedly, someone told Richard III that Edward IV's marriage to Elizabeth Woodville was illegal. This would mean the princes were not true heirs. Richard III seized the throne and the princes were never seen or heard from again. To this day, no one knows the boys' fate. But one person had good reason to get rid of them—their own uncle.

DID YOU KNOW? Written history declined in the 15th century. Works on philosophy and theology were also sparse. This plays a role in why it's difficult to solve mysteries from that time.

King Richard III's wife also met an untimely death. Some say Anne Neville died of disease. Others suspect that she was poisoned so Richard could remarry. If the new king was in fact responsible for the murders history suspects him of, then his looming karma was well deserved.

Richard III ordering the deaths of the princes

HOUSE OF LANCASTER HORRORS

Disturbing behavior was not just seen in the House of York. Margaret of Anjou, wife of Henry VI, was infamously vicious. After the Battle of Wakefield (1460) and a Lancastrian victory, Margaret demanded the heads of two Yorkists be displayed looking over the city walls of York. One head bore a paper crown. A sign alongside the heads read, "Let York overlook the town of York."

Richard III's son and only heir died suddenly of unknown causes. The king met his end at the Battle of Bosworth on August 22, 1485. He was the last English king to die in battle. More happily though, the end of Richard's life brought an end to the Wars of the Roses.

The Battle of Bosworth was the last significant battle of the Wars of the Roses.

MAKING CONNECTIONS

TEXT-TO-SELF

Do you think mysteries like the ones in this book are worth taking the time to solve? Why or why not? What can we learn from solving them?

TEXT-TO-TEXT

Have you read any other books about Cleopatra, King Arthur, or the Wars of the Roses? What more did you learn from those books?

TEXT-TO-WORLD

Do you know of any mysteries in history that were finally solved? How was it solved and who figured it out?

GLOSSARY

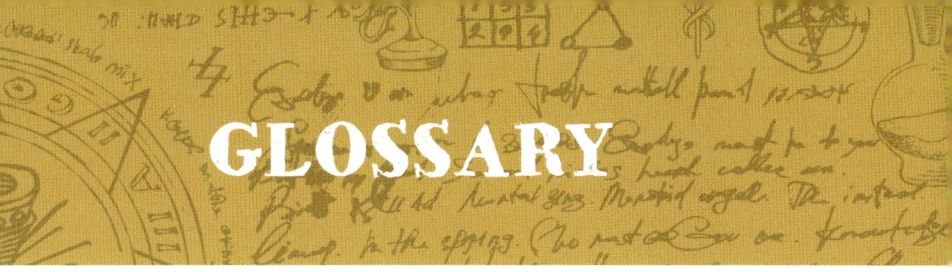

Anglo-Saxon — a person of Germanic descent who lived in England.

asp — any of several small, poisonous snakes found in Africa.

Briton — one of the people of southern Britain before and during the Roman times.

cavalry charge — an offensive maneuver in battle in which soldiers advance toward their enemy at their best speed.

coronation — the ceremony at which a king or queen is crowned.

hieroglyphic — a picture or symbol that stands for a word or sound.

mummy — a dead body that has been preserved with special chemicals and wrapped in cloth.

pharaoh — a ruler of ancient Egypt.

scholar — a person who has knowledge, usually gained from research and study.

INDEX

Anglo-Saxons, 16—17
battles, 9, 17, 28
Cleopatra, VII 6—12
Edward IV, 20, 24—25
Edward V, 25—26
Egypt, 5—12
Greece, 9
Henry VI, 20, 24

King Arthur, 14—20
Martinez, Dr. Kathleen, 11—12
Nennius, 17
Richard III, 24—28
Roman Empire, 9, 11, 16
Sword and the Stone, The, 17—18
Tower of London, 24—26
War of the Roses, 20, 28

ONLINE RESOURCES
popbooksonline.com

Scan this code* and others like it while you read, or visit the website below to make this book pop!

popbooksonline.com/anc-med-secrets

*Scanning QR codes requires a web-enabled smart device with a QR code reader app and a camera.